Advent
Christmas

Proclamation 3

Aids for Interpreting
the Lessons of the Church Year

Advent
Christmas

Walter Brueggemann

Elizabeth Achtemeier, series editor

Series B

FORTRESS PRESS   Philadelphia

COPYRIGHT © 1984 BY FORTRESS PRESS

Library of Congress Cataloging in Publication Data

Brueggemann, Walter.
   Advent/Christmas, series B.

   (Proclamation 3)
    1. Advent. 2. Christmas. 3. Bible—Homiletical use.
  4. Bible—Liturgical lessons, English. I. Title.
  II. Series.
  BV40.B76 1984   251   84–6020
  ISBN 0–8006–4101–9

K954C84   Printed in the United States of America   1–4101

Contents

Series Foreword

Proclamation 3 is an entirely new aid for preaching from the three-year ecumenical lectionary. In outward appearance this new series is similar to *Proclamation: Aids for Interpreting the Lessons of the Church Year* and *Proclamation 2*. But *Proclamation 3* has a new content as well as a new purpose.

First, there is only one author for each of the twenty-eight volumes of *Proclamation 3*. This means that each author handles both the exegesis and the exposition of the stated texts, thus eliminating the possibility of disparity between scholarly apprehension and homiletical application of the appointed lessons. While every effort was made in *Proclamation: Aids* and in *Proclamation 2* to avoid such disparity, it tended to creep in occasionally. *Proclamation 3* corrects that tendency.

Second, *Proclamation 3* is directed primarily at homiletical interpretation of the stated lessons. We have again assembled the finest biblical scholars and preachers available to write for the series; now, however, they bring their skills to us not primarily as exegetes, but as interpreters of the Word of God. Exegetical material is still presented—sometimes at length—but, most important, here it is also applied; the texts are interpreted and expounded homiletically for the church and society of our day. In this new series scholars become preachers. They no longer stand back from the biblical text and just discuss it objectively. They engage it—as the Word of God for the worshiping community. The reader therefore will not find here the divisions between "exegesis" and "homiletical interpretation" that were marked off in the two earlier series. In *Proclamation 3* the work of the pulpit is the context and goal of all that is written.

There is still some slight diversity between the several lections and calendars of the various denominations. In an effort to overcome such diversity, the North American Committee on a Common Lectionary issued an experimental "consensus lectionary" *(The Common Lectionary)*, which is now being tried out in some congregations and which will be further altered at the end of a three-year period. When the final form of that lectionary appears, *Proclamation* will take account of it. In the meantime, *Proclamation 3* deals with those texts that are used by *most* denominations on any given Sunday. It also continues to use the Lutheran numbering of the Sundays "after Pentecost." But Episcopalians and Roman Catholics will find most of their stated propers dealt with under this numbering.

Each author writes on three lessons for each Sunday, but no one method of combining the appointed lessons has been imposed upon the writers. The texts are sometimes treated separately, sometimes together—according to the author's own understanding of the texts' relationships and messages. The authors interpret the appointed texts as these texts have spoken to them.

Dr. Walter Brueggemann is Professor of Old Testament at Eden Theological Seminary, Missouri. Educated at Elmhurst College, Eden, and Union Theological Seminary in New York, he is widely known as a stimulating lecturer, scholar, and author. Among his books are *The Prophetic Imagination, The Creative Word,* and a commentary for preachers and teachers, *Genesis.*

ELIZABETH ACHTEMEIER

The First Sunday in Advent

Lutheran	Roman Catholic	Episcopal	Pres/UCC/Chr	Meth/COCU
Isa. 63:16b–17; 64:1–8	Isa. 63:16b–17; 64:1, 38	Isa. 64:1–9a	Isa. 63:16–64:4	Isa. 63:16–64:9a
1 Cor. 1:3–9	1 Cor. 1:3–9	1 Cor. 1:1–9	1 Cor. 1:3–9	1 Cor. 1:1–9
Mark 13:33–37 or 11:1–10	Mark 13:33–37	Mark 13:(24–32) 33–37	Mark 13:32–37	Mark 13:24–37

Advent does not begin in buoyancy or celebration or in a shopping spree. The natural habitat of Advent is a community of hurt. It is the voice of those who know profound grief, who articulate it and do not cover it over. But this *community of hurt* knows where to speak its grief, toward whom to address its pain. It remembers far back, behind the present trouble, the name of the God who presides over our hurt, who is Lord in the hurt, and who will bring it to a full end. And because the hurt is expressed to the One whose rule is not in doubt, this community of hurt is profoundly a *community of hope*. It hopes passionately that the trouble will end. And the end of the trouble will come when God returns to override the hurt and establish a kingdom of well-being for those who have endured and expressed the hurt.

The hope is concrete. It is as concrete as the hurt. Preaching at the beginning of Advent moves between those two realities of *hurt and hope*. Such preaching discerns that the two come together. There will not be one without the other. And it discerns that both are subversive in our culture because we are inclined to speak about our hurt no more concretely than we are inclined to express our hope. It is the reality of the present trouble that is the impetus for a vivid and relentless hope in these texts.

OLD TESTAMENT READING

The Old Testament text (Isa. 63:16–64:8) shows the waiting community become like a little child, abandoned, but not yet ready to be an orphan. The text is bound in 63:16 and 64:8 by the same bold assertion:

> For Thou art our Father,
>
> ....
>
> Yet, O Lord, Thou art our Father.

That much is not in doubt. The parameters of the text yield the parameters of Advent. We begin knowing whose we are. We are not abandoned orphans. Nor are we self-sufficient adults. We are children of this parent whom we have not seen as present lately but to the anticipation of whose coming we desperately and passionately cling.

Between the two assertions is a wide-ranging exploration of what it means to look to the abiding Father in the midst of trouble. The intermediate verses are mostly lament. V. 17 accuses God of abandoning and misleading. And it appeals for his return. V. 19 characterizes Israel's sorry present situation as though this had never been God's special people.

But such a sense of abandonment is not the end of the matter. Isa. 64:1–4 appeals for the coming of the Father to make things right. It remembers previous interventions which took us by surprise, interventions that have shattered the known world. Now the text waits for another coming like that. Then vv. 5–8 again present the sorry situation: "We have been in our sin a long time . . . we are unclean . . . polluted . . . faded, blown away . . . abandoned." And then comes a powerful YET (64:8). That "yet" is the basis of Advent, a *yet* against all the present data, a *yet* based only in the person of God in whom we hope and to whom we belong. It is an appeal that supersedes the circumstances all around.

The movement of the passage itself traces the motifs that provide entry into Advent:

> A 63:16 Thou art our Father
>   B 63:17–19 abandonment
>   C 64:1–5a The remembered coming
>   B′ 64:5b–7 abandonment
> A′ 64:8 Thou art our Father

The passage is ordered to move from a parameter of identity ("Thou art our Father") through the present trouble to the center in a remembered coming, which asserts a God *who works for those who wait.* In that ancient time, and in our time, only certain kinds of communities can *wait and hope.* They are those who know the name of God, who remember God's past action, and who understand God's cruciality for our life. It is they who embrace and live, without quitting, in the midst of abandonment. It is for them that Advent is accessible. The church community is a community that waits, remembering God while embracing present trouble, resiliently confident of a God who will "meet joyfully" the faithful ones.

EPISTLE READING

It is to that very community of hopers in Corinth that Paul writes (1 Cor. 1:3–9). The cultural community of Corinth was not much on waiting. We know it to have been a self-indulgent society, inclined to think that everything to be given is already in hand. Hence, there is nothing for which to hope. But Paul does not write to that general community of self-indulgence and self-sufficiency. To such people Advent makes no sense and offers no chance. Paul writes specifically to "those sanctified, the ones called to be saints." They have a different readiness, a readiness linked to the rule of Jesus. They know something and look forward to something the world can never expect.

So Paul writes in thanksgiving and joy for this little community (vv. 4–6) that has a different set of expectations. What he knows is that this community of the call has a distinctive way to be present in the world:

They are *those who wait* for the disclosure of Jesus Christ. We tend to think that in the New Testament, as distinct from the Old, there was no more hoping because in Jesus everything was already given. Not so for Paul. Christians who already knew the story of Jesus did not bask in everything being settled, but they waited eagerly for the disclosure of Jesus in all his fullness, that is, as the real ruler of God's new age, the one whose power takes the form of weakness.

The little flock that waits, *waits for the end* (v. 8). And God will stand by them until the end. We have found "end time" talk embarrassing or just irrelevant. But that is what Advent is about. It concerns the termination of the known world, the world of abandonment, grief, alienation, and injustice. Paul invites the church community in

Corinth to reflect on the end that is promised and is sure to come, when all the props on which we lean are taken away.

Then Paul makes his third and decisive statement: *God is faithful* (v. 9). It is a statement parallel to "Thou art our Father." Nothing else is reliable. All else will give way. Everything else will end. All who trust any other loyalty will be abandoned. This is the single abiding agent in the midst of the end to come. The urging of Paul to the Corinthian church is singularly in keeping with the elemental hope of Isa. 63–64.

The reality of God who is faithful (1:9) is that of the Father who abides in every circumstance (Isa. 63:16, 64:8). The anticipated end of everything, even what we treasure (1 Cor. 1:8) is likened to the hoped-for coming, which will be as decisive as the remembered coming (Isa. 64:4–5). The posture of eager waiting in 1 Cor. 1:7 is precisely the waiting for the one "who works for those who wait for him" described in Isa. 64:4. The elements of the drama are reiterated and become clear:

the end of the fragility of the present arrangement

the anticipation of a decisive turn

the centrality of God, who moves in the midst of these two elements.

GOSPEL READING

All the preceding prepares us for the third text, Mark 13:32–37. It is the Gospel reading, but it strikes us as very odd in the gospels. It is called by scholars the little Apocalypse, the miniature revealing. (Note that in 1 Cor. 1:7 there is reference to the "revealing," that is, the apocalypse.) Of all the gospel texts this one is most unambiguous about waiting for a coming that will be decisively disruptive.

The structure of the text is a threefold imperative:

> Take heed, watch (v. 33);
> Watch therefore (v. 35).
> Watch (v. 37).

This urgent imperative follows a text (vv. 14–27) that makes use of extravagant imagery. But these verses by themselves are sober and disciplined. They do not contain any bizarre suggestion but simply an assured affirmation that there is a coming "by the master," who will come to assert his rule. And in his coming heaven and earth, the known world, will pass away. The crucial thing is to be awake, alert. The ones who do not miss out are the ones who wait.

THE MEANING OF ADVENT

Now we are confronted with a claim in these three texts that there will be an end to the known world. That end will be brought by God alone. And our role is to wait expectantly, to be ready and waiting. That claim is not difficult to spot, and in one way or another it dominates all three texts. But it is an affirmation that is exceedingly difficult to engage, given our modern sensibilities. We seek a way into the text that, on the one hand, resists a decoding of the urgent message into a psychological formulation. (So we will not go the way of "demythologizing.") On the other hand, we seek a way that avoids the awkwardness of the literalists who speak this text flatly, with too much conviction, in ways that make no sense. The ground between obscurantism and modernization is not very great. Such a text must be approached cautiously, lest we say too much and therefore be too much misunderstood.

But this much is clear. Advent is not a "business as usual" festival of things we now know and now possess. It presents us with a strangeness that jeopardizes our world. The coming of King Jesus (which, of course, is our theme) is not an innocent baby who comes gently to fit into our preconceived world. No, the coming of Jesus is more like a master who comes at midnight, more like a God who stands with us to acquit us in judgment, more like a God who cracks open the human and causes the nations to tremble. Advent is about a shattering of the known world wrought by the power of God.

Advent is the shattering of all that we treasure. There is devastation and loss in his coming. Maybe the preacher has inadequate words to speak from God's side about this coming. Perhaps the preacher can only speak from this side, out of the fear and the dread which heavy loss imposes. That much we know in our time. We know about dread, inhumanity, about the terror of war, anxiety over collapse of the dollar, the selfish insecurity introduced by the oil shortage, the deep fear of the nuclear threat covered only by a veneer of civility. The shattering cannot be communicated in flat language but only by image and metaphor of the text itself, which cut underneath reason and play on our sensitivities. Advent is to make contact with those deep places our culture too much ignores.

But the shock of Advent is not just destruction. The text dares receive it also as a liberation. Advent means the shattering of the restrictive forms, of the shapes of oppression and paralysis that beset us and keep us from living half of what we would. The shattering is an odd thing, both *welcomed* and *dreaded*.

This is the news that will not be accommodated to our settled world. Perhaps the congregation will reflect on why such a notion is so alien to us. It is only partly our scientific purview. It is also our psychology of autonomy in which we seriously credit no outside agent. And it is in part our self-sufficient economy, in which we are accustomed to buying our way. But all that is now in deep jeopardy. For when our imaginative sensibilities are assaulted as they are by these texts, we begin to sense the connections and to ask about all the other parts, now seen to be linked. Then what can be salvaged? Who can be saved? The answer of these texts is, Nothing, in its present mode.

This is news that will not be accommodated to the settled world where all of us live. A sermon on such a subject runs in the face of settled wisdom. It is conventional wisdom, especially among those who merchandise Christianity, that we can buy and sell and share and trade within a settled world of care and fear, of profit and loss. It is conventional wisdom that God presides over this sure world to keep it benign and friendly toward us. We are seduced to the notion that we can have the world on our terms if only we work at it in clever ways.

Well, that is conventional. But it is not biblical, not Christian, not news. What we ready ourselves for in Advent is the sneaking suspicion, the growing awareness, the building restlessness that this weary world is not the one God has in mind. God will work another world. God will work it soon. God will work that new world according to the person and passion of Jesus. God will work a world precisely for those who are ready and able to relinquish the old one.

I am not sure how to preach such an assertion that falls outside our reasonableness, intellectual, psychological, and economic. Perhaps the best conceptual frame is the ''life-world'' of social network and symbol as understood by Berger, Luckmann, and Schutz. That means we may not be talking about the physical reality of earth ending but about the world of social possibility. And, in a kind of naiveté, that is perhaps what the text has always intended. Thus Advent asserts that our world of value and power and security is on its way out.

Advent puts the hard question. It shatters our presumed worlds. It meets us precisely where our hurt and our hope converge around the person of Jesus. It asks if we are bold and sharp enough to speak the hurt that belongs to us and to our weary world. It asks if we are ready and open enough for a newness to be given. It asks if we know the name of the Father to whom we belong, of the Lord whom we confess, of the coming one for whom we wait, and if we trust that one enough to relinquish the old world.

These texts could never have been very popular texts among people like us. They always must have been intellectually troublesome to people who can hold the world in their minds and see it whole. They always must have been religiously offensive to those who prefer a tamed piety. They always must have been deeply disturbing to those who love order, who can scarcely stand an abrasion or a contradiction, or who can never imagine a real ending to all that we treasure. The text jars us, invites us to leave the future ajar. Advent is for thinking through "not one stone left on another" (Mark 13:2). Nothing should be offered to tone down the dismantling. We dare only affirm that the dismantling is not done by an enemy, by a hostile one. It is done by "our Father," by the God who is faithful, by the Master whom we serve. We are asked if we trust that one enough to lean into an ending, perchance to meet the one who works for us.

The Second Sunday in Advent

Lutheran	Roman Catholic	Episcopal	Pres/UCC/Chr	Meth/COCU
Isa. 40:1–11	Isa. 40:1–5, 9–11	Isa. 40:1–11	Isa. 40:1–5, 9–11	Isa. 40:1–11
2 Pet. 3:8–14	2 Pet. 3:8–14	2 Pet. 3:8–15a, 18	2 Pet. 3:8–14	2 Pet. 3:8–15a, 18
Mark 1:1–8	Mark 1:1–8	Mark 1:1–8	Mark 1:1–8	Mark 1:1–8

In different ways these three texts speak about the hope we celebrate in Advent, a hope that is concrete and at the same time massive. The hope is concrete because it insists that God's utter newness is about to break upon us in ways that are specific and identifiable. The hope is massive because it is expressed in cosmic terms, about the turn of the world. The preaching opportunity is to make clear that what is going on with us is what is going on in the whole world, because God governs both.

OLD TESTAMENT READING

The text from Isa. 40:1–11 meets the listener in the midst of exile. These are Jews who have been deported to Babylon, forced to live under an alien regime and to accept its notions of reality. But it is not Babylonian pressure which makes all this exile. What makes the people exiles is that they refuse to assimilate, refuse to accept Babylon as home, refuse to credit Babylonian authority. Exile as a religious condition is not a result of oppression. Exile is a product of faith, deep faith which refuses to settle and which plants a yearning for homecoming. So the situation is met by God's word precisely at the point of this yearning for homecoming. This text at Advent articulates our yearning. It asks us to reflect on our "home," on our sense of estrangement and on our "Great Refusal" to whatever regimes falsely claim our lives. The poet of exile is here mandated by God to speak to exiles about homecoming. The internal event may be cultic (it happened in the sanctuary) or spiritual or psychological. That circumstance does not matter. What matters, according to the text, is that the "voice of heaven" authorized these words in the mouth of this human poet. The rest of us who stand before the book of Isaiah get to watch this commissioning service, to see clearly and unambiguously the authorizing, and to hear the words that are to be announced to the displaced persons who still yearn for home. The messenger authorized and the message announced point to this breathtaking reality:

> A highway is to be built halfway across the Near East, clear to Jerusalem, a highway to dramatize the extravagant coming of the King, King of Israel, holy God whose work is to bring exiles home. (v. 3–4).

> The King is said to have the power of a great decree (v. 8). He utters this homecoming word that is utterly reliable. Against it the empire is helpless even as Pharaoh was helpless at the Exodus. The power of the old regime is like grass. It will wither away (vv. 6–7). The old world yields to the decreed homecoming.

> Then comes this awesome formula of enthronement: "Behold your God" (v. 9)! See the real King, just crowned, excluding all pretenders to power.

The exiles hear the message. They are forced to decide which word they believe, which regime they serve, either the tired regime which keeps us enslaved, or the new King who brings us home. It is the work of the gospel (and of the preacher as gospel bearer) to show exiles the true God, to show that this God warrants our trust.

GOSPEL READING

What strikes one as most crucial for the drama of the text from Mark 1:1–8 is that it still concerns John the Baptist. We are still "pre-Jesus." Jesus is for Christmas. But Advent belongs to John. It is for hope and waiting and expectation. And it is for turning loose old loyalties.

Mark begins his story by calling it "gospel" (v. 1), that is, news about the end of the age, the intrusion of the new age. And the *cosmic* reality of the new age is identified with the *historical* reality of Jesus. The theme is announced. This appeal is made to the memory of *exile and homecoming* (vv. 2–3). The remainder of the text focuses on John,

who is the last abrasive voice of the old age but also the harbinger of
the newness to come. Advent may mean thinking about the *work* of
John, the *person* of John, and the *words* of John.

The *work of John* is to baptize (vv. 4–5), an act giving access to the
new age. We have so domesticated baptism into a private act that we
miss its claim as a public transformative act. It refers to dying and
rising to the new kingdom (cf. Romans 6:1–11). The substance of this
act is identified in two phrases. First, there is *repentance,* turning
loose of the old age and all its loyalties and values. It means rejecting
the absolutizing claim of the old regime. Each preacher will have to
decide about what this means in a particular setting. But if the
metaphor of Babylon is still operative in this text, then I suggest the
loosening of the old age may refer to the consumerism of our culture
which besets us and enslaves us. Advent may be a time for thinking
through a refusal of that regime, an unambiguous no to whatever it is
that enslaves. Second, there is *forgiveness,* that is, release from old
debts. The debts may be economic, but we are also deeply obligated in
terms of our spirit and our imagination. Our whole human capacity for
newness has been largely co-opted. Forgiveness of sins should not be
trivialized. It refers to release from a whole system of indebtedness
which keeps us from being human or by which we manage and ad-
minister other people.

The *person of John* is characterized as an outsider (v. 6), as one who
comes from the wilderness and has dressed the part. Not only is he
geographically an outsider; he has kept his distance from the seduc-
tive good things of his culture (cf. Mark 8:15). He comes as a raw,
abrasive person to speak out of another world of freedom which has a
different angle of vision. And so he dares call for an end to conventional loyalties and attitudes. John in his person enacts the liminal
situation which we experience when old forms of life are in question
and new forms are not yet clear. Advent is such a threshold moment. It
is an occasion for embracing uncertainty, for pondering the am-
biguities that let us make new decisions and understand ourselves
differently. Thus John's person matches his work. He invites us into
an open space where new mandates and fresh assumptions may be
experienced. The dominant old regime that is all about us will resist. It
will want us well-fed (not on locusts and wild honey) and well-dressed

(not in rough camel's hair) and well-housed (not in the wilderness) in order that we do not depart from old loyalties. We are "kept," and the old order wants to keep us so. John's person reminds us that there is more than one way to live in this world. (See also Matt. 6:25–33 on these seductions and the offer of an alternative way.)

John's words (vv. 7–8) point beyond himself, beyond the dangerous moment of transition. John is like Moses who points across to the new land but does not enter it. He anticipates the edge of newness. But he does not name Jesus. Christmas is time for naming Jesus. But Advent is a time for unspecified waiting and hoping. What John knows is not the name of the person but that it is the work of the Spirit which will blow open the world and permit a newness that staggers (v. 8).

John's articulation is an urging for *spiritual* reconstitution. But the linkage to Isa. 40:1–11 keeps his work specific and *political*. Those who hope for the kingdom are always exiles in the old age. The point is preachable in our time because increasing numbers of people experience displacement in the system, cynicism about its trustworthiness, and a yearning for something more and something other. Here it is about to happen!

EPISTLE READING

I suggest a sermon from the epistle reading might focus on two facets: First, it is promised that the full kingdom will be established. It is promised as firmly as Isaiah promises homecoming or as John promises one greater. The Christian community gathers around that promise, certitude undiminished by the delay.

In a scientific culture it will be important to see what the notion of *promise* might mean. We are wont to reduce promise to prediction. But promise is speech in another idiom. It speaks about the intent of the speaker, not the mode. It transcends time and is not enslaved to a chronology, being either "a thousand years or a day" (v. 8). It allows the speaker great latitude and counts unambiguously on the reliability of the one who makes the promise. Conversely, it invites the promise-trusters (that's us) to trust the promise, to grasp for no other certitude, to conjure no secondary causes. Promise is a mode of relationship which gives both parties freedom and asks for a kind of trust that is not subject to verification. Perhaps the most important theme of Advent is the awareness that gospel realities have to do with promises. That is, they are made for freedom, slippage, loyalty, all qualities alien to our orderly, quantifying, controlling society.

The promises are kept in ways we do not expect and cannot resist—their coming will be like a thief (v. 10). The thief does not come on schedule, nor in publicly planned ways, but always sneakily. "How silently, how silently, the wondrous gift is given." The thief works in silence. But things are changed. We find we are robbed of the old world and, it is to be hoped, left open for the new age. So the preacher invites the congregation to observe concrete moments in which the new way of gospel does surface, in political acts, in destitute pain, in liberated speech, in healing gestures. We must not miss them.

But the promise pertains not only to personal and casual matters. It says that the whole old world will be dissolved (vv. 11–12). The "coming again" will utterly displace the way things are. As the Babylonian empire could be "dissolved" in one generation, so we know that the oppressive regimes among us and within us will be dislodged. It is promised! It is promised that an end will come to the war system, the greed system, the injustice system, and all those spinoffs of hurt, loneliness, fear will go as well. It is promised, and therefore sure.

Second, the text is not much interested in cosmic speculation. It rather focuses on ethical preparedness. Given such promises, how shall we be ready to receive them? Christmas is about cosmic transformation. But Advent is for ethical preparedness. As at no other time, there is in this season a yearning for "betterness." And the church must not shrink from helping people make the most of that yearning and that possibility.

Begin with the marvelous phrase "waiting and hastening" (v. 12). This is a phrase taken up by the Blumhartds (father and son), German pastors who cared passionately for the marginal people in their society. Ethical preparedness includes eager longing, trusting in a new world, never growing cynical that it has not yet come. *Hastening* means to act with passion, to act as if the rules of the new regime were already in place. "Waiting and hastening" bespeaks the rhythm of a prepared life, knowing that everything is in abeyance and not in our hands, leaving it to God, and yet being relentless in moving toward it.

Preparedness means "holiness and godliness" (v. 11). The words are almost too large, so the preacher has lots of liberty. But in our context I suggest *holiness* means to be utterly devoted to the promises God is about to keep, and so to be increasingly disengaged from the old world, which is pregospel. It is an acute pastoral question whether "relevant" people can be so devoted to God's promises. But perhaps it is time to reverse that issue and to claim that the only relevant people are those waiting for God's fullness. All the others are irrelevant because they are beholden to the Babylonian regime, which can keep no human promise. Perhaps to be either/or is too simplistic. But a summons to repent makes such a demand (v. 9). It eliminates the middle ground of indecision. The pastoral task is to think through with the community what new life might mean.

In reference to "without spot or blemish" (v. 14), the writer uses the language of the priestly cult of Leviticus. It refers to offering animals that are not marred or made unworthy to God in sacrifice. The image urges Christians to keep their lives acceptable to God (cf. Rom. 12:2). The image perhaps cuts two ways. One way is *moral integration.* Obviously people who "waste" their lives cannot receive promises. The other way is *eschatological alertness,* so that the "blemish" may not be a moral deficiency, as judged by the world, but to be hopelessly settled in. If this interpretation is correct, it may suggest it is as unacceptable to be cynical as to be an adulterer. The phrase being "holy, acceptable to God" refers to being transformed and not conformed. There is a rich Advent theme stressing disengagement from the values around us which render us disqualified.

Finally, we may be "at peace" (v. 14). Even in our frantic culture, Christmas is enacted as being "at peace." The traffic stops. The shopping stops. People take time. There is for us an instant when the Babylonian system looses its power. And that moment is not to be mocked. It is like a sabbatic gesture.

But the text means more. It means that those who wait for the kingdom will be reconciled to brother and sister, that there will be a time for healing, forgiveness, for starting again. And since we are enmeshed in a political and economic system that relies on war to solve problems, to be at peace means to be thinking about dissolving the system. Thus ethical preparedness is not limited to personal inclinations but concerns the shape of public life.

The Third Sunday in Advent

Lutheran	Roman Catholic	Episcopal	Pres/UCC/Chr	Meth/COCU
Isa. 61:1–3, 10–11	Isa. 61:1–2a, 10–11	Isa. 65:17–25	Isa. 61:1–4, 8–11	Isa. 61:1–4, 8–11
1 Thess. 5: 16–24	1 Thess. 5: 16–24	1 Thess. 5:(12– 15) 16–28	1 Thess. 5: 16–24	1 Thess. 5: 12–28
John 1:6–8, 19–28	John 1:6–8, 19–28	John 1:6–8, 19– 28 or 3:23–30	John 1:6–8, 19–28	John 1:6–8, 19–28

By this third Sunday in Advent we are able to discern a repeated claim in this set of lections: A *cosmic transformation* is promised. It is embodied in *the historical person of Jesus*.

The texts *summon the community to joy*. The ground for joy is not yet fully present. But it is on its way, fully and surely and close at hand. In the Isaiah text it is an announcement of "good tidings," (v. 1), comfort for the mourning (v. 2), gladness to replace mourning (v. 3), and at the end of the poem, rejoicing and exultation. In the Pauline statement of 1 Thessalonians, it is much more cryptic: "rejoice always." That is all.

THE MEANING OF JOY

The sermon may help the congregation think through what it means to rejoice. It seems rather obvious. But things need sorting out in the harried euphoria of the Christmas season, when we sing about joy but many face staggering depths of depression. Our culture generates a frenzy, and the church can do some sorting out.

We may observe that joy spoken of here is not the same as pleasure, nor satiation, nor even the emotional high we call happiness. It is rather a steady assurance of the resolution of the incongruities, an assurance that those contradictions may be sloughed off by what is about to happen. This is not delight in possession of something, but in passionate anticipation for what is not yet in hand.

The congregation may be helped to see that joy is not a mark of our culture. One can discern that by watching folk, especially in this season in the pushing and shoving of a shopping mall or any other place else where people have their guards down. Most people look bored or distracted or tired. And boredom, distraction, and fatigue are not helpful conditions for joy. Joy is an active enterprise linked with dance and song, not an emotion of the bored or exhausted. Let us observe that this text is addressed to a social setting in which real joy is a rare practice among us.

In these texts the community of faith, a minority community, is invited to the scandalous, subversive activity of joy. This community is authorized to do something the dominant culture is unable or unwilling to do. While the large community prefers its sorry weariness, this community is invited to an alternative way in the world. Joy, genuine Christian joy, undermines frantic activity. It shakes us free from the world that controls us by keeping us tired. And the ground for this alternative action is that something special, not yet widely known in the world, has been disclosed to us. These texts *announce a fundamental transformation of reality.* That is the reason for joy. Here we are at the center of the text and the center of the gospel.

TRANSFORMATION OF REALITY

The change is articulated in Isaiah 61 in quite concrete terms. It is *news,* unexpected, inexplicable: the crushed are healed, the debt-slaves freed because debts are cancelled, the prisoners released; there is a general amnesty. The constriction of a frightened world will yield—soon or late. Crushing moralism will not stop human liveliness. Dreams of freedom will not be silenced by totalitarianism. Dreams of justice will indeed come to fruition, in spite of inequitable public institutions.

The *mourning* here (v. 3) is not for a private death. It is because of public oppressiveness, in which folks despair that their lives are in hock. But there will come "salvation"—read "liberation" (v. 10).

There will come "righteousness," that is, making all equitable in a world that seems crushingly uncaring. The world is transformable and will be transformed. I do not spend time here trying to make a convincing case, trying to make the claim "reasonable" because the text does not. That is because the claim is not reasonable. We will never be reasonably persuaded about such an astonishing claim. It can only be proclaimed; it cannot be argued. We must first free our imagination so that another way of thinking and seeing and knowing can be practiced in our world. We are not aiming here at different conclusions, but at different presuppositions.

The congregation does not need to engage in speculation about ways or modes or times. It is enough to ponder the substantive claim of the rule of King Jesus. It will displace present power arrangements. That is why we celebrate in anticipation. The church's anticipation of "the coming of our Lord Jesus Christ" is not an empty, formal claim. It takes its substance from the concrete memory of the historical Jesus. The coming cosmic transformation which we celebrate is known in the concreteness of Jesus:

> the blind receive their sight, the lame walk, lepers are cleansed and the deaf hear, the dead are raised, the poor have good news preached to them (Luke 7:22).

What Jesus has done, Jesus will do. This we celebrate.

THE WORK OF THE SPIRIT

The transformation to be celebrated is known to be the work of God's resilient Spirit. The work of the Spirit is evident in these texts in various ways. It is most explicit in the Isaiah passage (61:1). All that follows from this text is wrought by the Spirit. It is the Spirit that authorizes and empowers the speaker to undertake transformative social acts. It is the Spirit that initiates the moves that lead to comfort (v. 2), to restoration (v. 4), to rejoicing (v. 10), to righteousness (v. 3). It is the Spirit who makes newness where everything is hopeless.

In 1 Thess. 5:19, the reference to the Spirit is terse. But if one examines the entire epistle, it is clear that the Spirit is seen as the power which has formed this community and which continues to energize it. So the gospel has come to this congregation in the Spirit

(1:5). It is the Spirit that brings joy, even though in affliction (1:6). It is the gift of the Spirit from God that marks this community (4:8). That is, it is the Spirit that makes the church the church. It is the Spirit that gives faith, that causes caring, that permits hope. It is the Spirit that makes this community exceptional and noteworthy, distinct from its worldly context which is dis-spirited. It is no wonder that Paul admonished, "Do not quench the Spirit," that is, do not resist or squelch that power that has marked the life of the church.

In the gospel lesson, reference to the Spirit is not explicit. But the statement of John 1:28 is half a statement. In the church tradition preserved in Mark 1:8, Matt. 3:11, and Luke 3:16, the other half marks the coming of Jesus, the one who will baptize in the Spirit.

The texts and, indeed, the early church's claims about the Spirit are not easy to systematize. And they should not be. It is enough to recognize that these texts speak of "the Force," the resilient, free power of God to work an utter newness in a world which seems closed to God's impingement. Perhaps the best part of John 1 for this motif is that it seems to refer back to Gen. 1:2. There it is the Spirit of God which blows upon the chaos to make creation. Now the same wind from God blows to authorize a liberation (Isa. 61:1–3), to form a new community (1 Thessalonians 5), to initiate a new age of "light." The "Spirit" is a way the Bible speaks of newness from God which is not at all derived from anything presently available in the world. It is for the Spirit that transforms, that the church waits in Advent. The tired, closed world finally will not be able to resist.

JESUS: EMBODIMENT OF THE SPIRIT

Though the Spirit is a gift from God, the evidence of the Spirit is in a *concrete, identifiable historical agent.* Advent in the church is not anticipation of a universal or cosmic "glow." It is waiting for the appearance in the earth of an agent engaged in mission. We do not wait in general. We wait in particular.

In the Isaiah text the speaker is not named. But he is a specific human agent sent on a specific mission. And the church's use of this text (cf. Luke 4:18–19) is prepared to identify that enspirited agent of liberation precisely as Jesus of Nazareth. That concreteness is of course stated in the gospel reading. The entire text points to "one whom you do not know." Jesus is not named. But his identity is not in doubt. In the epistle, there is a waiting for "the coming of our Lord Jesus Christ." The church waits for none other.

This one who comes in Christmas is a cosmic Christ. Of course. And the claims are very large. But the claims for the cosmic Christ drive the church back to our memory of Jesus of Nazareth, and that Jesus of Nazareth is not the baby of piety but an abrasive liberator, who empties the prisons and overturns the debt system (Isa. 61:2–3), who overrides all the old conventions and creates new possibilities, who liberates and heals, and who finally becomes such a threat he is killed.

Out of these first four points, we may draw a focus for preaching: The church *rejoices;* the church rejoices over a decisive *transformation;* the church rejoices over a decisive transformation *wrought by the Spirit* in the historical person of Jesus confessed to be the Lord who comes.

It is the juxtaposition of transforming Spirit and historical person which is the difficulty of preaching and the glory of Christmas faith. It is precisely *cosmic* surprise become *concrete* that permits joy.

RESISTANCE TO THE GOOD NEWS

We may suggest a final point that is perhaps tenuous but that we believe is there in the text. This assertion of joyous transformation *evokes resistance.* We image ourselves ready for Christmas. But there is an abrasion, because this coming means the end of our known world. We are reluctant to relinquish what we have known and controlled and lived from.

In Isaiah 61, there is no resistance to the good news. But when the text is taken up in Luke and assigned to Jesus, there is enormous anger:

> All in the synagogue were filled with wrath. And they rose up and put him out of the city. . . . (Luke 4:28–29).

I think the same beginning of resistance and opposition is hinted at in John 1:24. The Pharisees here are not yet hostile. But the Fourth Gospel already anticipates the attitude which will lead to hatred and conflict (cf. John 15:18). The Pharisees do not come to receive but to question. They hope to get enough data to slot the new movement into some category of the old order. And as the Gospel unfolds, the contrast of new wine/old wine (John 2:10) and the invitation to be born again (John 3:5) are judgments on old patterns of faith. In Advent we must face that the coming of the new King leads to joy but also to hostility. It is a welcome newness and an unwelcome shattering of all our models of managing our known worlds. The problem is that this is one "whom you do not know."

THE COMMUNITY OF JESUS

What can one preach here? It is clear that in these texts there is such a richness that no sermon could comprehend it all. One could preach on one or more of the themes outlined. Or one could preach on one of these texts according to this general movement. My own inclination would be to focus on the epistle because it is the freshest and least familiar and because it makes a move from Jesus (Christology) to church (ecclesiology). We are inclined to focus on Jesus in this season. This text reminds us that Advent is *anticipation of the new community* in the world, wrought by the power of Jesus, mandated by the way of Jesus, and living toward the hope of Jesus. I do not by that mean to reduce the hope of Christmas to the church. Rather, I mean to suggest that the person of Jesus presses us to think about the *people of Jesus*. This text is an opportunity to let the congregation think through what the new King means for this community. The verses of 1 Thessalonians 5 preceding our reading (vv. 12–15) offer quite practical admonitions about how to order the community. It is an invitation to relate in very different ways in the community, that is, "See that none of you repays evil for evil, but always seek to do good to one another and to all" (cf. Matt. 5:43–48, Rom. 12:21). Then our reading (vv. 16–24) gives the ground and basis for this new community:

This community *rejoices* because it knows the grip of old modes is broken (v. 16).

This community *prays and gives thanks* (v. 18), that is, its whole life is directed toward God. There is a total yielding of self-interest.

This community is energized by the very Spirit of God, an energy devoted to *behavioral responsibility* (vv. 21–23).

This community *hopes and waits* with great discipline (vv. 22).

The text envisions a church fully reshaped by the move of the Spirit. Such a sermon would keep us from generalizing about Christmas and would keep us from romanticizing about individual experience. Newness comes *to* community and *as* community.

The Fourth Sunday in Advent

Lutheran	Roman Catholic	Episcopal	Pres/UCC/Chr	Meth/COCU
2 Sam. 7:(1–7) 8–11, 16	2 Sam. 7:1–5, 8b–11, 16	2 Sam. 7:4, 8–16	2 Sam. 7:8–16	2 Sam. 7:1–16
Rom. 16:25–27	Rom. 16:25–27	Rom. 16:25–27	Rom. 16:25–27	Rom. 16:25–27
Luke 1:26–38	Luke 1:26–38	Luke 1:26–38	Luke 1:26–38	Luke 1:26–38

For this last Sunday prior to Christmas we are given texts, all of which have to do with *speech* which is abrupt, unexpected, decisive, and world changing. The three speeches do not have much in common. But if one wants to hold the three texts together in one sermon, the best possibility may be to consider the intrusive speech of the gospel which changes life. Then one can begin with the expected focus in God's speech to us in Jesus Christ (word become flesh) and move backward and forward from there.

GOSPEL READING

The Gospel reading (Luke 1:26–38) is of course well-known. But the evangelical claim of the text is often missed because of a rather mechanical focus on "the virgin birth." We may begin by observing that this is a greeting (v. 28). It is an odd, unsettling greeting from a stunning source which gives a new reality to Mary's life.

Observe the source of the greeting. It is from Gabriel, messenger from God. The narrative on the one hand treats this intrusion rather routinely, as if an angel belongs in a story just like Herod or Zechariah or Simeon. And yet in an understated way the narrative wants us to see this is no ordinary speech. It intrudes into the routine world of the woman. It brings news that transforms forever everything in her life.

The substance of the greeting is a birth announcement. It is the initiation of a new season in the life of Mary, and a new age in the life of humanity. Extraordinary means (an angel) are used for extraordinary content. No doubt this is a most unusual birth. That cannot be disputed in this text. But the uniqueness of "virgin birth" belongs in a narrative which is unusual in all its parts, not just the biological part. We are already on notice about that because of the messenger Gabriel.

But the narrative does not linger over the bold claim of virginity. What takes up the major portion of the text is a characterization of the child to be born. That poetic blessing by Gabriel is in two parts, divided in v. 34 by Mary's question. The first characterization (vv. 32–33) is *an enthronement speech*. This is king talk. The scandal is political, not biological. The surprise is that the new king is born to peasant folk in a place as unnoticed as Nazareth. This is talk of throne, reign, kingdom. The language is Davidic, claiming all those old promises. And it is theonomous, showing all this to be from God. Yet it is speech to unnoticed, marginal folk.

In v. 37 the narrative draws the unavoidable conclusion: nothing is impossible for God—not a virgin birth, not a new beginning, not a king among peasants. The verse echoes the question to Abraham and Sarah in Gen. 18:14. Now the question is answered. That is precisely the Advent question awaiting the answer of Christmas. The news is an impossibility now become possible.

We may observe Mary's response to this assault on her known world. In v. 29 she is *troubled* because the initial greeting is unlikely. In v. 34 she is *perplexed* at the impossibility. But in v. 38, at the end of our text, she *accepts* the word, acknowledges her identity in relation to the Lord, and *submits* herself to the unreasonable announcement. In v. 45 she is celebrated by the narrator because she trusts the promise.

The text invites us to ponder how the inscrutable newness of God can have its say with us. I suggest the preacher must not flinch here from the virgin birth. But the bold claim of that birth must be understood as the evocation of a new way to be present in the world. The reality of virgin birth does not occur in a vacuum. It is odd and noteworthy that the "fact" of virgin birth is often defended precisely by those who want the world most rigid, closed, and ordered, that is, those who want no real newness. Here virgin birth is not a mere *fact*. It is *news,* a word about something new which shatters the whole old world. And if the ready response of Mary is our model, then Mary is celebrated, not because she believes in biological miracles, but because she submits herself to God's impossibilities and trusts that God's promises will come to shattering, surprising fulfillment. The Lucan text does not linger over a biological oddity but asks about an alternative history that is initiated by nothing more substantial than a promise and that from an angel.

OLD TESTAMENT READING

The promissory language of Luke 1 looks back to David, and especially to our second reading, 2 Sam. 7:8–16. This text, a staggering promise to David, is perhaps the pivotal text in the faith of the Old Testament. It also is an unwarranted speech which changes historical reality. It is not borne by an angel, but its deliverer is equally inscrutable as it is a disclosure from God, given in the night (v. 4). Again the narrative wants to make the point that this is not "reasonable" talk and it cannot be explained. The oracle is discontinuous with the known, administered world of David. In that regard, this dream speech is not different from the preceding angel speech. Both bear words which cannot be from the world already at hand, but are ways in which the fresh, free purposes of God can become known and visible.

The speech is of interest to us because the language of this text was found useful by the early church. This does not mean the text in its inception referred to Jesus. But it has become the source of much messianic expectation and has been an important point of departure in thinking about the trusted and promised king whom God will give.

The text again assaults the known world (vv. 4–7). In vv. 1–3, the known world seemed sure and guaranteed. In the first instant, David wanted to build a temple because that is what successful kings always do, and God, at first, gives authorization (v. 3). On that basis, nothing is exceptional or noteworthy. But apparently God has second thoughts. In this dramatic turnabout, God has decided not to participate in the standard religious convention (vv. 4–6). God asserts a surprising distinctiveness. This God will not be a God like all the other gods. This God, unlike the others, is free, on the move. The break made here on the part of God is at least as radical and important as the break caused by the virgin birth. Indeed, the whole story is a recital of discontinuities.

So instead of being the God who *receives* temples and accepts worship as an object of adoration, this God resolves to be the one who *gives* life, who guarantees David, who authorizes the dynasty and who permits a temple. Note the drastic inversion—not the object to be adored but the subject who intervenes and makes all things new. The historical recital of vv. 8–9 is the story of taking a nobody and transforming him into someone important. If virgin birth in Luke 1 be only a biological fact, then there is no linkage. But if it be a political inversion, then we may suggest that this miracle of David is as radical and displacing and amazing as the birth of Jesus.

In the remainder of the text (vv. 1–16), the narrative looks forward. It imagines a future for David and for David's family which will shift the ways of power, reorganize the life of Israel, and make things newly ordered and secure.

The most crucial promise, no doubt, is the one in vv. 15–16. V. 15 asserts that the giving of covenant loyalty to David's family is irrevocable. Nothing can make God withdraw. And v. 16 is a dynastic promise that is unconditional and abiding, said to be "forever." Note that the same "forever" is articulated in Luke 1:33, in the poem which also sounds dynastic.

The thrust of the speech is of course to the future. What a future! It is a future upon which the early church seized (as in Luke 1:69), seeing in David the promise of life and well-being and liberation now come to fullness in Jesus of Nazareth.

The decree of this chapter is pivotal for Jews and Christians. It is a root text for all messianic hope. The text cannot be tied too closely to Jesus. And yet, given our historic appeal to the Old Testament, it cannot for us be detached from Jesus. What we do know is that God's fulfillments always outdistance God's promises. Jesus outdistances David (cf. Mark 12:37), and our hopes out of this text run well beyond all the promises to new fulfillments.

This text is a life changing, power authorizing decree. The point is not argued or explained. It is simply asserted. But in this assertion, everything has been changed. David at midlife becomes someone he has not been. The shepherd boy (1 Sam. 16:1–13) has become shepherd over Israel (2 Sam. 5:2). New possibilities are made available precisely because God breaks free of old arrangements and does a remarkably new thing.

EPISTLE READING

Our third text, Rom. 16:25–27, is also a world changing speech. In some ways this is a very curious text to group with the other two. The texts from 2 Samuel 7 and Luke 1 fall together easily. But not this one. It is a blessing or benediction formula placed at the end of the letter. We may presume it belongs to the standard repertoire of benedictions in the early church. Moreover, the author of the speech is different. The first two texts were disclosed respectively by an angel and in a dream, whereas this is human speech, likely stylized in a liturgical way. And the placement is different. Luke 1 is the beginning of something new, the birth of an impossibility. 2 Samuel 7 is a promissory decree in the midst of David's life, which is completely transformed. But this one comes at the end and gives closure. So perhaps something can be made of an end speech to match the beginning speech of Luke 1. Perhaps one might say the life of faith is bracketed between the invitation to impossibility which begins things (Luke 1:37) and the summons to praise which closes things (Rom. 16:25–27).

The benediction itself, though brief, is enormously complicated in its rhetorical structure.

The beginning and end of the blessing formula refer to God: Now to him . . . to the only wise God. . . . The speech invites the church (at Rome and now here) to refer its whole life to God in praise. This befits the argument of the letter to Rome, for the whole argument has been that human life and human hope derive, not from us, but from God. That is a useful Advent note. The coming of Christmas is God's singular action, and in this festal season our lives are to be referred to God alone.

If we take one step inward from the two references to God in something of chiastic fashion, we find two covenantal themes that appropriately belong together. On the one hand, this God is praised as one able to strengthen us (v. 25). That of course is what the whole gospel is about, the God who transforms weakness to strength. That is God's covenantal commitment evidenced to David, the weak shepherd made strong king. It is for that Paul would give thanks, for power made perfect in weakness (cf. 2 Cor. 12:9).

On the other hand, the move to the center of the text from v. 27 to v. 26 concerns command and obedience to the faith. The God here praised is the one who gives unconditional promises but who also calls for unqualified obedience. The Advent season is a time in which the church thinks again about its hopes and how those hopes provide the ground for radical obedience.

The means by which this God is able to strengthen and by which this God calls to obedience are expressed in the center of the benediction in vv. 25b–26. Here the words almost tumble out, and we might linger over each one: "gospel . . . preaching . . . revelation of mystery . . . secret disclosed." Paul understands very well that what is celebrated as strength and obedience is not something perfectly obvious and generally known. In that sense, our anticipation of Christmas is not an event of civic life, even civil religion. It is a peculiar piece of news, known among us but not known generally. That revelatory mystery, that secret entrusted to some, is the gospel known in Paul's preaching. And we know from elsewhere that Paul's gospel and Paul's preaching about Jesus have to do with the cross and with the reality of Jesus' crucifixion.

So the claim made here is that God on High is to be praised for the decisive disclosure made in the crucifixion of Jesus. This preaching will tax the preacher in the midst of American Advent. Our preaching has not to do with commonly held popular religion but with a secret that contradicts, namely, that God's way of transforming the world is by the cross, which then calls and empowers the church in the way of the crucified to the obedience of the cross. But such a conclusion should not surprise us. The other two texts have hinted at it. In Luke 1, we have suggested that virgin birth is not simply a biological miracle but a political inversion. And we have seen in 2 Samuel 7 that in rejecting the temple, God has broken with conventional royal religion. Now the mysterious secret that evokes response is not a big public victory but a disclosure of weakness inviting distinctive praise.

God is to be glorified. Of course. That is what all the carols articulate. But the glory of God is not a conventional epiphany. It is a glory through Jesus Christ, the weak, crucified one. So the Advent theme of birth-promise looks ahead. It invites the preacher to comprehend the whole life of Jesus, evoked in a scandal and characterized as a humiliation. It is that kind of glory of which angels sang at Bethlehem, a glory unlike standard royal birth, unlike standard royal temple, unlike all of our masterful conventions.

The ones who glorified God had to respond. Each had to embrace a deep displacement in life:

So Mary had to face and live with impossibility and is credited with trusting its fulfillment.

So David had his attention turned from temple building. He was no longer permitted by the voice in the dream to do conventional things. He had to find a new way to be king.

So Paul yielded the secret that brings about obedience to faith, perhaps the obedience he so boldly characterized in chapter 12.

The texts might permit the church to discern something most important—Christmas, God as word become flesh, is not what the world thinks. It is rather an invitation to reorganize our life together around words that nullify old presuppositions and securities. The invitation of the texts is to be open enough to receive the new King in ways that are appropriate to his dangerous rule. It is a secret made available to us that we sometimes, ignorantly, are too eager to receive.

The Nativity of Our Lord, Christmas Day

Lutheran	Roman Catholic	Episcopal	Pres/UCC/Chr	Meth/COCU
Isa. 52:7–10	Isa. 62:11–12	Isa. 9:2–4, 6–7	Isa. 62:6–12	Isa. 62:6–12
Heb. 1:1–9	Titus 3:4–7	Titus 2:11–14	Col. 1:15–20	Titus 3:4–7
John 1:1–14	Luke 2:15–20	Luke 2:1–14 (15–20)	Matt. 1:18–25	Luke 2:1–20

These lectionary selections deny the preacher the usual birth narrative for this day. That will be missed in the congregation by some who want the festival to be conventional. But it provides an opportunity for a more reflective, meaty sermon about the evangelical claims of Christmas. Each of these texts is rich enough by itself. But here I suggest a movement through the three of them.

OLD TESTAMENT READING

Isa. 52:7–10 is an announcement of hope to exiles. It is placed in that part of Isaiah dated to the sixth century exiles in Babylon. And the announcement is that the Lord's governing power is now to be enacted in a way that will permit Israel to go home. The actual dramatic shape of the text features two key figures. The first is a messenger who runs over the desert terrain from Babylon to Jerusalem with a special message about a turn in world events. He comes breathlessly toward Jerusalem with news they can hardly believe. Events in Babylon have changed so that it is clear that God is indeed sovereign. For a long time it had not seemed so. But now the Babylonian gods who had seemed so invincible are defeated and discredited, not trustworthy, not able to do what they say. The formula, "Your God reigns" (not some other god), is a formula used at a coronation to acknowledge the powerful claims of this particular God.

The second set of actors in the drama is the watchmen on the city wall of Jerusalem. The people in Jerusalem had been hopeless and in despair since the destruction of 587 B.C. There was a deep malaise. There still were watchmen on what was left of the walls (cf. Isa. 21:11–12). Partly they were there to guard, but partly they were there hoping for a messenger with news of a change. In v. 8 the *watchmen* spot the *messenger* from exile. They can tell by the way the messenger runs that the news is good (cf. 2 Sam. 18:24–27). They anticipate the coming of victory news and the reestablishment of the Lord's rule.

In v. 9 they charge the despairing people in the ruins to celebrate the return of God from exile. V. 10 gives the reason. God has shown his power among the nations. That means new power and possibility for the people of God.

This text is both hope-filled and exile ending. The preacher must work at two awarenesses at the same time: To be clear about *the reality of exile*, which may only be clear as homecoming is presented; to be clear about *the expected homecoming*, which may only be clear as exile is embraced. We will not know about the powerful possibility of home until our situation in exile is made clear. We cannot celebrate that new possibility unless we see it in contrast to our situation of alienation. And mostly we lack enough awareness to see either as it pertains to us. Preaching from this text at Christmas time is therefore unsettling because it articulates a God who is free in contrast to our present arrangements, and it asks us to think through our own situation in which we are too "at ease" (cf. Amos 6:1) in a false peace into which we have been seduced. That is, the values of Babylonian imperialism and the happy seductions of our culture have no easy peace with this Gospel.

EPISTLE READING

Heb. 1:1–9 is an announcement of quite specific hope, namely, hope in Jesus. This may strike us as an odd text at Christmas. But it makes an important point. The hope of Christians, the hope at Christmas, is not just a warm, vague, good feeling. It is precisely hope in Jesus and in none other. And that is sobering.

In the beginning of the letter, our reading makes a staggering assertion about the uniqueness of Jesus. Notice, however, that Jesus is not named until 2:9, not at all in the first chapter. For the first chapter we have high, eloquent talk about "the Son," but that is a royal title that still lacks concreteness.

This text provides opportunity for considering Jesus in some detail as the focus and embodiment of Christian hope.

He is heir of all things (v. 2), that is, all the promises of God in the Old Testament are aimed at him. All the "hopes and fears" of Israel and humanity are met in him.

Through him God created the world (v. 2). This text antedates the great dogmatic formulations of the church creeds, but here already an ontological claim is made that the Son is a preexistent agent of the primal act of creation.

The Son reflects the glory of God and bears the very stamp of his nature (v. 3). This verse moves fully in the direction of claiming Godness for Jesus. The birth celebrated in this day is the enfleshment of none other than God. So the festival is much more than the romantic arrival of a baby. It is a decisive turn in the character of creation, for the agent of creation has now come as part of creation.

Characteristic of this letter, the writer makes an enormous claim that is alien to much modern psychologism and historicism. It is the articulation of a faith that might sound old-fashioned to our minds that have emptied the gospel and have settled for a Christology of "moral example" or "good friend." The text asserts much more, that the order of reality is now irreversibly modified.

The text exerts a great deal of energy to contrast Jesus with the angels. Thus in v. 4 Jesus is superior to the angels. In vv. 5, 6, 8 God says things of Jesus he would never say of angels.

Now the point is clear. But in our context it would not seem to carry much weight. What could this mean in a congregation that has not believed in angels for some time? If we do not believe in angels, then it is not much of a claim to say that Jesus is greater than angels.

At best this is difficult. We must try to seek what our contemporary equivalent for angels might be. Angels are agents of God, gifts of God given to us by God for our well-being, faithful to God's purpose, but far enough removed from God that they are never reckoned as capable of giving salvation. God bestows them as gifts that are welcome but not sufficient. So in v. 7 (a reference to Ps. 104:4) the wind and lightning are God's angel messengers, bringing newness but not full embodiments of God's power.

So the preacher must ask, What are the welcome gifts of God that are not sufficient to save but are nonetheless valued gifts? In our day this might include technology, standard of living, scientific knowledge. Each of these is welcome to us. Each of these makes us grateful to God and is a way God blesses us or at least holds the potential for blessing us. But none of these is able to save. Indeed, when we credit saving to our technology, for example, we engage in idolatry. For what we are imagining is that any of these other gifts from God could do God's saving work. Angels—of whatever identity—are glorious creatures if kept in perspective. But when too much is assigned to them or expected of them, we shall be misled, and we shall fail to understand the distinctive claims of Christ. So the text is at pains to make a distance and a distinction between Jesus and any other would-be source of salvation. Christian preaching now as always insists on Jesus alone, denies all of the would-be alternatives that eventually become idols. The text is a doxology, but it is also a reassessment of rival claims.

The contrast is established by an extended and imaginative treatment of Old Testament materials, now all related to Jesus:

V. 5 quotes from Ps. 2:7, which is a coronation formula.

V. 5 quotes from 2 Sam. 7:14, a dynastic promise that is to perpetuity without condition.

V. 6 quotes from Deut. 32:43 and perhaps from Psalm 97. A bold move now reassigns doxologies originally directed to God to Jesus.

V. 8 quotes from Ps. 45:6–7. The text is not completely clear. Though it appears to be addressed to God, it could have been addressed to Israel's king. But if the latter were so, the verse expresses a very high view of kingship.

This very learned arrangement of texts is designed to assert that all possibilities now rest with Jesus. There are no religious hopes or resources other than those linked to Jesus.

Now we may reflect on the preaching problem here. The claim of the distinctiveness of Jesus will be offensive to a kind of tolerant faith in much of the liberal church which is not quite resistant, but certainly reluctant, about such a claim. But if rightly understood, the distinctive claim for Jesus may be equally an affront to comfortable conservatives who easily mouth faith in Jesus but tend not to take Jesus singularly but along with prosperity, certitude, and moral self-satisfaction.

GOSPEL READING

John 1:1–14 is a familiar text which further articulates this Jesus who is the source of new hope. This text by itself of course is so rich that we cannot explore its resources. In relation to the other texts, I suggest two preachable points:

The movement of the text is from the completedness of heaven to the riskiness of earth. The movement itself carries the message of an evangelical intrusion. There is a beginning point *with God*. The end point is *among us* (v. 14). And the hinge point is "he came" in v. 11. Neither *with God* nor *among us* by itself is news. What is news is the invasion from out beyond us, from the throne of God, which radically reshapes the darkness. Structurally then, this text expresses the same movement as Isa. 53:7–10. It is an announcement of one who comes in power among the ruins to make all things new for exiles, for inhabitants of darkness.

But what I want most to stress is what is asserted about Jesus. Three dimensions make this Jesus the goal of our hope:

First, he is one who is *not received* (v. 11). Now that is a burden to preach at Christmas. But it is the scandal of the gospel. The Jesus who comes does not accommodate himself well. That must be pondered. The very people who hoped finally got the one for whom they hoped, and they rejected him. Why? Because he came in "flesh," (v. 14). That means not only in earthly form but in weak, vulnerable form. The cross already looms large in the first verses of the Gospel. The coming one is not a triumphant, but an "empty" one. Our hopes are sure to be disappointed by Jesus if our hopes are shaped by the success syndrome of our society or that of the messianic tradition. What is hoped for is not quite what is received.

Second, the weak, fleshly one who is something of a disappointment is the one with *real power* (v. 12). Jesus is seen to have power. But it is not usual power. It is power the world rejects because it is the wrong kind. Jesus' true power is not to make things right or prosperous. It is only to let us be who we are created to be—children of God. And how are we empowered to that? By weakness. We confess that this fragile Jesus has the capacity to transform life. And the whole of the Fourth Gospel shows that the one who washes feet is the one who gives life (13:8). It is the empty one who makes full (Phil. 2:7–8). It is the poor one who makes rich (2 Cor. 8:9).

We ponder the two points: *powerful* (v. 12) yet *rejected* (1:11), because his power is a strange and embarrassing kind that lets us be transformed for the purpose of the Gospel.

Third, this rejected, powerful one comes full of *grace and truth*. The two words are the Old Testament formula, *ḥesed and 'emeth,* loyalty and reliability. And that finally is what might be hoped for and celebrated on this day. A new calculus is here introduced into our world. The loyalty of God in Jesus countermands the handy, easy throwaway detachment of our society. The faithfulness of God contrasts with our daily experience of betrayal, for this God betrays no one. No wonder the angels sing of glory (v. 14, Luke 2:14) as do we—"gloria in excelsis." But it is not the glory of imperial Rome or expansive America. It is the glory of the rejected one, now known to have power of a new kind.

It is not easy to preach this concept at Christmas, for it suggests a message alien to our holiday expectation. I think I would try to state the odd juxtaposition of *hope* and *Jesus,* for they have a strange relationship to each other.

Recognize negatively that *hope* and *Jesus* are odd companions. There are people who hope, but they do not seem to trouble with Jesus because Jesus is perceived as irrelevant to the buoyant, who expect newness to come out of *our* life. Conversely, there are those who believe in Jesus but who do not hope because Jesus is perceived simply as one who endorses and guarantees the present. Such may be the religious zealots who have taken Jesus as a moral power without disruptive authority. Or they may be the secularly indifferent who take Jesus as a good idea in general but manage to fit him into a previously arranged world.

The truth of the Gospel is this: *we hope because we believe in Jesus.* It is in Jesus that we have the embodiment of intrusive newness. It is the strange power and lingering fascination of Jesus that cause us to expect something yet from God. What we hope for from Jesus is that we should become children of God. The remainder of the Fourth Gospel tries to characterize this hope. It is the hope that we, like Nicodemus, will be permitted to start over as children. It is our hope that we, like Lazarus, may be dead but restored to new life and freed from all that binds us.

The coming of Jesus into our world may help us focus on this profound yearning that we should become who we are meant to be. But it is more than a yearning. It is a gift of power to have it so. We are here authorized and permitted to become free of whom we have been, children of some lesser god who gives neither grace nor truth, neither loyalty nor reliability.

The hope we have in Jesus is a hope that *conforms to Jesus' way in the world.* The Jesus received is not the one expected. He is one who embodies and summons us to a new dangerous faithfulness. The coming of Jesus meets us with a dangerous choice. We can become transformed by the power of the gospel to be God's folk, walking in God's vulnerable ways. Or we can reject him and continue business as usual. The latter means to stay in the shambles and ruins of old, defaulted Jerusalem (as in the tradition of Isaiah). It means to remain in the darkness apart from God's will. But it need not be so. The story around which we gather is a transforming hope for a new life. The text invites and permits new beginning. Where that happens, heaven and earth do sing, there is joy to the world, the waste places do break forth together in singing. But it means the end of the life and world into which the Word has not yet come in shattering fleshly ways.

The First Sunday After Christmas

Lutheran	Roman Catholic	Episcopal	Pres/UCC/Chr	Meth/COCU
Isa. 45:22–25	Sir. 3:2–6, 12–14	Isa. 61:10—62:3	Jer. 31:10–13	Isa. 45:22–25 or Sir. 3:2–6, 12–14
Col. 3:12–17	Col. 3:12–21	Gal. 3:23–25; 4:4–7	Heb. 2:10–18	Col. 3:12–21
Luke 2:25–40	Luke 2:22–40 or Luke 2:22, 39–40	John 1:1–18	Luke 2:25–35	Luke 2:22–40

These texts aim at the connection between the birth of Jesus (Christmas) and the possibility of newness (New Year). They permit us to ask what Jesus has to do with newness. The Sunday after Christmas is in any case a problematic Sunday. Given the cultural trappings of our holiday season, there is more fatigue and depression around than there is any inquiry about newness. Beyond the trouble of the season, ours now is a culture that either in pride or despair does not much look for newness. So Jesus instead is contained and made to fit our present schemes. With these texts at this moment in our liturgical life, the preacher may ponder how this ancient Jesus can impinge upon a season of transition.

GOSPEL READING

I assume these texts are focused on the Gospel lesson, which is one of the few narratives we have in the gospel account that relates to the birth events and yet looks beyond to the next moves in the life of

Jesus. So the most obvious connections are to begin with the Gospel reading. The text makes the move we must make in the aftermath of Christmas. Luke 2:22–24 provides a transition which summarizes the standard action of going to the temple. This text seems almost like a byproduct in the total narrative. It reports what seems to happen quite routinely. And these two people (Simeon and Anna) are the first in the world to recognize the distinctive claims of Jesus, thus anticipating the greater epiphany yet to come. They are credited with seeing in faith first. It is their "eyes of faith" which let them see, for there are as yet no active, visible clues available to them.

I suggest this text permits a reflection on a theme "piety confirmed and shattered." The narrative presents two pious people, Simeon (vv. 25–35) and Anna (vv. 36–38). (Vv. 39–40 are a concluding summary which corresponds to the introduction of vv. 22–24 and need not detain us.) We may consider each of these in turn. First, Simeon:

Vv. 25–27 characterize the preparation for this recognition. They suggest that Jesus does not enter into a vacuum but that he comes into a predisposed context. The piety of Simeon is a form of readiness, and we might reflect on piety as the receiving ground for Jesus. Simeon's readiness consists in two elements. First, he *hopes*. And his hope is quite concrete (v. 25). He anticipates, expects, and waits for the comfort of Israel. That is, he looks for the end of exile and displacement that has been a longtime mark of his people (cf. Isa. 40:1). He believes that things need not and will not stay this way. Sooner or later, there will be a new future that overrides the present despair. His hope is not specified except that Messiah is mentioned (v. 26). His hope may have been for a political triumph.

But, second, it is clear that this is not enough. For a new baby is hardly an agent for a political triumph. The other factor in his readiness is that Simeon is subjected to, invaded by, guided to recognition *by the Spirit*. Three times (vv. 25, 26, 27) it is the Spirit who breaks the piety of Simeon, so that the shape of his hope is broken. He continues to hope, but now he is led to see that right hope is of a kind and in a form he had not understood. Pious waiting is crucial. But even that needs to be transformed. God gives even as we expect. But God does not give what we expect.

So the actual disclosure of vv. 28–35 is not what standard piety hoped for. In Simeon we are offered a portrait of an open person who is genuinely surprised and profoundly moved by what is given in this new child. We may ask, How did he make a connection between this little baby he holds in his arms and the great hopes of salvation about which he speaks? How did he recognize who this is? The answer of course is that it was by the Spirit that he made the linkage. Simeon here is like Peter later who also recognized who Jesus is. And, when he properly confesses Jesus, he is told, "Flesh and blood have not revealed this to you, but my Father who is in heaven" (Matt. 16:17). So also with Simeon and all who keep Christmas.

This text thus focuses on an acute pastoral question. Of all the confused and competing religious claims, how do we know that this innocent, vulnerable Jesus is the clue to all reality? The text does not invite obscurantism or a refusal to think things through. But it does anticipate an openness to surprise. It is affirmed that the key to the whole process of history (in Israel and beyond) is not in kings and empires, not in learning or in power, but in this Jesus who never appears, if we judge with the eyes of the world, to be that extraordinary.

Nonetheless, Simeon makes the confession that the whole church is invited to make. In this Jesus we have now disclosed to us our last, best hope. There is nothing after Jesus that will displace him. This does not mean there will be no newness. It means rather that we have made a decision, a decision that comes upon us with overriding force: the normative disclosure has been made. It is this new baby who dominates the scene. From this normative disclosure certain things follow:

First, there is a personal assurance (v. 29). Simeon and his company can return home with the deepness of life now satisfied. The yearning has been ministered to.

Second, we now know how the salvation/liberation of God's world is to be wrought (v. 30). This Jesus is the means of world transformation. There is no speculation about how this is to be. At this moment there is no curiosity about means and strategy.

Third, this transformation applies as well to the Gentiles (v. 32). We may observe that Luke throughout his account portrays this news to people not of the household of Israel.

And, fourth, this transformation contains within it the well-being and enhancement of Israel (v. 32). In this irenic story the liberation of

Gentiles and the exaltation of Israel are not in tension. Both are offered in new ways by this staggering child now in the midst (cf. Gal. 3:28).

Simeon's concluding statement to Mary is somewhat enigmatic (vv. 34–35). It seems to suggest at the same time that Jesus is the norm and instrument of judgment to come, that there will come tribulation on Jesus and those around him. Jesus' coming is a sorting out. As some will be blessed, some also will be harshly dealt with. As there will be blessing, so the coming of Jesus entails a rejection of others. But what comes clear in any case is that there is an abrasion between Jesus and the needful world around him. Jesus will not easily fit into the world he enters. He causes an unsettlement wherever he is. As we receive the Christ child into our context, we may be equally sure he does not readily accommodate. Where Jesus governs there is a sorting out, "a rising and falling." The last statement of v. 35 is especially odd: "the thoughts of many hearts revealed." I suggest it affirms that where Jesus is Lord, the world that has been *closed* by power and fear is now *dis-closed,* so that the hurts and dreams of the heart which have been censored and denied now receive a fresh hearing and a healing.

The second portrayal of piety, more briefly offered, is that of Anna (vv. 36–38). The name "Anna" derives from the Hebrew word for "poor." That fits with the characterization of the woman. She is an old widow. This means she is surely marginal and socially disenfranchised. She is the stereotypical one who finds life in the temple her genuine home, because she has no other. This portrait also announces an important theme in Luke, for his good news is precisely to the poor, the ones most needy, the ones most open, and the ones who have least ground for resistance. One would not want to tie it too closely, but this picture of needful piety in Anna might be a foreshadowing of the "poor widow" (21:1–4) whom Jesus acknowledges to give an acceptable offering. Especially in the Gospel of Luke, the pious poor are the ones who continue to hope and are able to receive. And they are regularly contrasted with the full, the powerful, and the successful, who experience Jesus mainly as a threat (cf. the summary statement of 19:47–48). The pastoral chance is here to help people reflect on new dimensions of piety which might let us be open to the innocence of Jesus.

Anna's response in v. 38 is that she offers exactly all that she is able to offer: *thanksgiving* (a word used only once in the New Testament). Her thanks is because she has discerned what only the pious poor might discern, that in the poor man of Nazareth has come the rescue of Jerusalem (cf. Luke 10:23–24). Who would think that the rescue of this great city would come through such a poor man? Certainly not the rulers of this age, of the state, of the church, or of the economy. For such people always think rescue will come in splendor, either the splendor of power or of money. But this woman knows. Luke places great trust in the perceptive power of the poor, the ones who discern who Jesus really is. So if this poor woman anticipates the woman Jesus saw giving at the temple (21:1–4), she stands as a model for those who worship rightly, for she "puts all her living" into her faith (21:4). What that text condemns are those who practice their faith, or embrace Jesus "out of the abundance." It gives us pause to see that in Luke it is those who have no abundance who draw close to Jesus and who see him for who he really is. We are asked who we must be in order to see rightly about Jesus.

OLD TESTAMENT READING

If we take these texts in sequence, first the Gospel and then the Old Testament reading, we encounter the Old Testament reading in the context of the hopeful poor who have received Jesus. This text in Isa. 45:22–25 is addressed to exiles. It invites them to embrace the Lord as the source of homecoming and thereby to reject all other ways of living in Babylon.

The text is a summons to submit, placed in the mouth of God:

> Turn to *me* . . .
> . . . .
> I am God. . . .
> By *myself I* have sworn,
> from *my* mouth
> . . . .
> to *me* every knee shall bow
> only in the Lord, it shall be said of *me*
> . . . .
> in the Lord. . . .

The rhetoric is a torrent of self-asserted claims that the door to the future for Israel is in obedience to God. That is the only prospect for homecoming.

It is not explicit in these verses, but the text clearly includes by implication the counter theme, *reject other gods,* quit trusting in alternatives that have no power to save. In the first instance this call for rejection refers to the gods of Babylon, who legitimized the oppressive empire. In 45:16, the idols are mentioned, and in the text that follows (46:1–4). The Lord, the living God of deliverance (vv. 3–4), is sharply contrasted with the gods of Babylon (vv. 1–2) who have no power to save and are in fact an added burden that have to be dragged along.

The text proposes nothing less than a "switch of gods"—the decisive rejection of other gods and the embracing of this God. That suggestion will sound strange to us in a culture that imagines our world is monotheistic and these are all the same God under different names. The point is not to quibble about the names or number of gods. The point is rather to determine who a god is, what a god does, and who are the natural allies of a particular god. In Babylon, in the New Testament, and generally, the gods who claim us mostly turn out to be allies of the empire, who *legitimate* oppressive order. The argument made here is that the distinctive mark of this God is that this one *liberates.* Israel is invited to submit to the God who liberates from all the legitimated oppressors.

Such a choice may sound strange, but Christmas is exactly a decision to "switch gods," to receive the God first visited by shepherds and regularly embraced by the poor, who knew instinctively that the gods of the empire are not real friends.

Rejection of Babylonian gods and embracing this Lord of liberation is the summons of the text. But our usage in relation to the Gospel reading means to give this summons a christological tilt. Thus we may say that the God to whom we are to turn in our exile is the Lord Jesus. That is the reading given Isa. 45:23 in the Pauline hymn of Phil. 2:10. The deference to be accorded God is here assigned to Jesus. Or, if one does not want to make such a direct christological designation, it is enough to see that the God embraced in Isaiah 45 is the one to whom Jesus decisively points.

The exiles of Isaiah 45 are to align themselves with the only God who can liberate. That is exactly the judgment that Simeon and Anna made in Luke 2. They understood that in this new child they looked upon the only one who could console Israel (Luke 2:25), who would redeem Jerusalem (Luke 2:38).

Now the tricky thing is such preaching is to articulate enough critical awareness, so that the congregation is also able to see what is at issue in our situation. It will be easy enough for us to conclude that we are not in exile waiting homecoming. We are not the poor in Jerusalem awaiting consolation. And anyway, we have embraced this God long before Christmas.

But Christmas poses the question afresh. It asks us not to name the name (cf. Matt. 7:21–23). It asks us to look anew at the theological commitments out of which we live and to discover that we worship a God masquerading in the name of the liberating one but who is largely on the side of power and order that oppresses, who is seen as a legitimator of the status quo, not one to whom the poor can turn with any hope of change. The business of "switching gods" may be more urgent, more abrasive, and more problematic than we can face. Most of the time we are rather innocent of the gods to whom we have submitted, regardless of the name under which they travel. This summons to submit is an invitation to reorder our loyalties, to abandon old trusts in prospect of a new life.

EPISTLE READING

The Gospel reading reports a dramatic embrace of this new "wedge of hope" in the world of Jesus. The Old Testament reading is a summons to submit. The epistle reading of Col. 3:12–17 nicely follows with a "So what?" What difference would a switch of gods make? The answer is that it leads to a new kind of life. *Fresh faith,* it is promised, leads to *new obedience* in the world.

This text reflects a genre of baptismal instruction in which baptism is treated in the metaphor of changing clothes, taking off old clothes and putting on new ones (cf. Eph. 4:22–24). The metaphor of changing clothes is overlaid with "dying with Christ" and "being raised with Christ to new life" (cf. Rom. 6:1–11; Col. 3:1–4).

Our text is the invitation to be *raised to new life,* to "put on" (vv. 12, 14). And this is preceded by the twofold negative, "put to death"

(v. 5), "put them all away" (v. 8). So the baptismal formula is symmetrical:

Die with Christ:	*Be raised with Christ:*
put to death (v. 5)	put on compassion, kindness (v. 12)
put away (v. 8)	put on love (v. 14)

But of course our concern is not formal. What is presented here is the new life of obedience that is embraced when Jesus is received as the consolation of Israel, the light to the Gentiles, and all other gods are rejected. Christmas is a time for "switching gods," a time to begin living differently.

The catalog of characteristic attitudes and actions here sounds like that which Simeon and Anna might practice. It pictures a life so open to the power of Christ that it has no need to dominate, to deal quid pro quo but can be a means toward transformed relations. Vv. 12–13 focus on *forgiveness* as a means of breaking the deathly cycle of vengeance and retaliation among us. Vv. 14–15 follow with an invitation to *agape and peace* which let the community have harmony. And the third element is to *be thankful.* The word is used three times: be thankful (*eucharistoi*) (v. 15); say with thankfulness to God (*chariti*) (v. 16); give thanks (*eucharistovtes*) to God the Father (v. 17). The new life which emerges from switching gods is marked by forgiveness, love, and thanksgiving. This behavior may be contrasted with the usual ethic of this age—retaliation, calculation, and resentment.

On this first Sunday after Christmas it will be difficult to sound this note of the new life. But what better time, while the church is still clothed in the joy and innocence of the Christ child? Christmas is not an orgy; it is a decision that the poor of God have made about a calling in the world.

It will strike us immediately that an ethics of compassion, kindness, lowliness, meekness, patience is quite a vulnerable way to live in the world. But these qualities are not rooted in romanticism. They are rooted in the vulnerability of God, who took this way of an innocent child to overcome the rulers of this age, to immobilize Herod and finally to undo Ceasar. God in God's own self has given like the poor widow, not out of abundance, but out of the very risk of life.

The ethic enjoined here is a dangerous one. I think that the Christian preacher in this festival of peace has an obligation to see about this ethic on a public scale, for Christmas is indeed a public event. There is a tendency at Christmas to be maudlin, especially about ethics. But we shall have to ask about this ethic as a public possibility in a public world of nuclear weapons. Such a bold proposal simply overwhelms all silly discussion of "red and dead," and reminds us that we have switched gods and now must switch ethics. Such a way seems not to include much 'Niebuhrian realism.' But the overriding realism is that practiced by Simeon and Anna and all exiles moving toward home. There is an invitation here for new hope, new piety, and a new ethic. The alternative is to live "out of our abundance," which fates us to keep the old gods and the old exile.

The Name of Jesus (January 1)

Lutheran	Roman Catholic	Episcopal	Pres/UCC/Chr
Num. 6:22–27	Num. 6:22–27	Exod. 34:1–8	Eccles. 3:1–13
Rom. 1:1–7 or Phil. 2:9–13	Gal. 4:4–7	Rom. 1:1–7	Col. 2:1–7
Luke 2:21	Luke 2:16–21	Luke 2:15–21	Matt. 9:14–17

The lectionary readings for this special day appeal to an old liturgic festival that celebrated the "circumcision of our Lord." Only very recently has this come to be related to the naming of Jesus, which alludes to the act of circumcision in relation to the naming. And thus the readings point to the name *given* Jesus and to the name *given us,* the people of Jesus, that is, those who bear Jesus' name in the world as a mark of faith and discipleship. It is appropriate that the festival of the name should come on New Year's Day, for the act of naming signifies a new person, new identity, new calling.

My central proposal is this: To gather around the name of Jesus lets the fundamental assurance of our life function as a beginning point of certitude and obedience, not as a conclusion lately drawn, which closes things off. That is, the Christian life does not labor anxiously, not knowing about the outcome until the last moment. It begins with the clarity of identity and call already guaranteed and in place. We do not journey doubtfully *toward faith,* but boldly *from faith.*

In the beginning of a new year we do not need to wait until the end of the year to see how it will come out, for we know about the basics even as the new year begins. The fundamental factors concerning our life in the world are already secure. In that certitude we are freed from anxiety to a life of freedom, openness, obedience, and risk.

GOSPEL READING

The Gospel reading (Luke 2:16–21) provides the movement from the event of birth (theophany) to the embrace of call (obedience). Before this point in the text we have had the lyrical, majestic statement of the "visited birth" (vv. 9–14). And, for all our familiarity with the story, it still catches us and leaves us stunned. We know without doubt that we are at a new beginning, powerful and inexplicable. After this text, we are met with procedures of purification (vv. 22–24), and by the end of the chapter Jesus is portrayed as facing into his vocation (v. 40). This transitional moment is to go from the energizing event of theophany to the sober, enduring reality of call.

The actors in this moment of transition are the shepherds. They represent for Luke all the poor who gladly receive Jesus. They are filled with amazement (v. 18). They must go back home (v. 20), but they do not go home the same. They return changed into voices of doxology (v. 20).

Luke shapes the Gospel narrative so that at the beginning point *doxology for the name of Jesus* (v. 21) is the clue to the whole story. The new year, the new gospel, the new life is about Jesus, the one who saves, frees, liberates, and transforms. And that is what the praise is all about. This lyrical affirmation of Jesus is formalized in the act of circumcision. It is an act of identification and belonging. The role and person of this "new one" are fixed for all time, fixed in the historical process of the Jewish people, fixed in the lyrical voice of the church, fixed as the linchpin of hope and joy for all people who begin new life and new year in the certitude of this reality.

We note well that Luke did not tell his gospel version so that we had to wait to find out. We do not need to wait to the end of the story to see how it comes out. We do not need to wait for mighty acts or authoritative teaching or even Good Friday or Easter. Everything is known at the outset. This new one is identified, and all of life is marked in a new and certain way.

At the beginning this community of faith does not need to wait to see about the year. We care, of course, about inflation and unemployment, disarmament, medical diagnoses, and interpersonal realities of hurt and healing. But our life does not consist in adding up the ledger on all this at the end. Our life is decisively shaped before we do anything specific. For the name of Jesus is not a conclusion drawn at the end. It is a doxology we speak with the shepherds at the beginning. We sort out the rest in light of our having already glorified God. The act of circumcision gives ritual verification of the name and the reality already authorized from heaven. Jesus is given a vocation. The shepherds find Jesus and find a summons to a life of praise. And so do we.

OLD TESTAMENT READING

In the Old Testament reading we have a second familiar text, so familiar that we hardly think of it as a biblical text, but only as a rubric during which the organist prepares the response and we are fidgeting in the pew, consolidating for departure. The long custom of the church is to put this benediction at the end of the service. That makes sense because at the end of the service we depart back into the world even as the shepherds must go back to work.

But I think very often that the Christian church spends much of its time, liturgically and dramatically, once again arriving not at the end, but at the beginning. It is like going to a three-day meeting of Christians, the culmination of which is the Eucharist. How much better would it be if the Eucharist were at the beginning to establish and affirm the baseline of fellowship, from which the community then reflects on its life and mission out of that baseline. That is what happens when this benediction is given as a reading, not at the end of the year, but at its very beginning. We begin with some things very clear and certain. The primal certainty is that we are blessed and given a new name.

It could be so if this passage were used to begin. Regularly and repeatedly the Christian community uses this text at the end of liturgy to establish once more the blessing, assurance, and well-being of the community. But how very different if occasionally this benediction were used at the beginning of a liturgical event so that the reflective time of the congregation were spent in moving *out* from this assurance. It would be analogous to the shepherds singing praise and glorifying God at the beginning of Jesus' life, not at its end. Perhaps the lectionary committee had something like this in mind in placing this text here, at the beginning.

The specific verses of the benediction are well-known to us. A benediction, or a blessing, is an odd form of speech. Probably it has evolved out of a wish so that the lines of the text could be rendered in the optative mood, "May the Lord bless," meaning "I hope so." But our understanding more likely is, not wish, but verdict and assurance, so that the lines are handled as an indicative. Thus they are pronounced with priestly authority, with the best established authority available in the community, which announces the true situation.

It is announced that the Lord *will bless,*

will give what is needed for life;

will keep. The text may be taken with reference to Psalm 121. The one who keeps this faithful community does not slumber or sleep but is always attentive toward Israel.

will make his face shine. This is a rather primitive metaphor which assumes that to see the face of the king is to be assured well-being. And conversely, if this God hides the face (cf. Gen. 4:14, Exod. 33:14–15, Ps. 13:1; 51:11), there is neither life nor hope. That metaphor seems odd in our individualistic culture. We can hardly imagine a situation in which the king is so all powerful that to be denied "audience" is equivalent to death. But that is what is assumed. To be granted an audience, to get to see the face, is an assurance of life. Perhaps the claim is understandable if, when we are in great pain, we are told, "The doctor cannot see you until next Thursday." Indeed, *seeing* the doctor and *being seen* by the doctor is the key point. Or to change the figure, a little child who has displeased her mother knows what it is to be "banished from the presence" (read "face") of the mother and wants only to be restored to the face, to the presence, where there is life and communion again.

will be gracious, that is, will act freely and not with calculation toward the worshiper, so there is no awkward question of merit.

Finally, the Lord's face is lifted (v. 26). There is an acknowledgment which gives life, and there is an assurance of *shalom,* well-being. It is clear that all parties assume that peace comes only from this single source, which has power to deny but generosity which gives. It is a blessing that does indeed let life begin again. To begin the year in benediction is no small gesture. God's generosity can be counted on to change our life at the very beginning.

That benediction is of course well-known. But v. 27, a part of our reading, is less well-known. "They shall put *my name* upon the people Israel." The benediction is in fact a festival of the name of Yahweh (the Lord). Each major element (three times, in vv. 24, 25, 26) begins with the name. The name Yahweh is used *doxologically* to celebrate this God. It is also used *polemically* to refute and deny the claim of every other god. So in that ancient world one might read, "The Lord (and not Ba'al) bless you and keep you." The benediction *asserts*. It also *dethrones*. What is accomplished is that this liberating, saving, healing name is laid upon Israel, and it changes and focuses the life, destiny, and vocation of Isreal. It is an act that in another setting serves the Israelites well. In the time of 2 Isaiah there were exiles who almost forgot who they were. And they were reminded:

I have called you by name—you are mine (Isa. 43:1). Thus the benediction gives identity, issues vocation, ends exile. It is no wonder that this text is set for the festival of "the name of Jesus." The name "Jesus" means "save." And this ancient priestly formula is a salvific assurance. It lets the people proceed—at the end of worship, at the beginning of a new year—marked in a special way, claimed for a special call, ready for uncharted living, not needing to be fearful, and not needing to accommodate.

EPISTLE READING

Perhaps the most important thing about the epistle reading (Rom. 1:1–7) is that it is at the beginning of the letter. That is, the premise for the letter is stated, so we are once again at the beginning point in making the decisive announcement from which all else follows. This paragraph of greeting is an exceedingly convoluted statement, in terms of literary construction, by Paul. But it can be identified according to the genre of ancient letters. Thus in form Paul follows a convention in three parts:

The first part is the most extensive (vv. 1–5). Stripped to its basic intent, it simply identifies the writer of the letter, Paul. But what follows makes clear that Paul is completely subordinated to his subject, the gospel. Paul is simply an agent (apostle) of this gospel. It is the gospel (and not Paul) that claims authority in what follows.

Paul is at pains to characterize fully the one to whom the gospel refers. He is accounted Son, from David according to the flesh, designated Son of God, risen from the dead, and finally the name is named: "Jesus Christ our Lord." Paul makes the claim upon which the whole gospel rests that is heard in the church. The text is clearly more specific than either of the other readings, and here the preacher has a chance to reassert yet again the decisive claim of the gospel embodied uniquely and fully in this single reading. Note that when the name is named (v. 4), it is then asserted that the ministry of Paul and of the whole church is to bring about obedience "for the sake of the name." It is the name of Jesus that is the ground, reason, power, and goal of obedience. The obedience enjoined, as Paul makes clear in the letter, is not adherence to a set of rules, but it takes Paul's most powerful imagination (Romans 12) to make clear what that obedience should be.

In vv. 6–7b the addressees of the letter are identified as those who are called to belong to Jesus Christ, the believers called to be saints, that is, the fellowship of the church. The newness here pronounced is not a general claim said to be true indiscriminately among the citizens of this age. The new beginning in the gospel is precisely for the church which stands under the name. This sermon at the beginning of the year thus is an opportunity to be specific and concrete about the call to mission in the church, to sort it out from general religious claims. That is important in a culture where a faithful church is likely to be a precarious minority.

The substance of the message between Paul and the church is in the first instant the brief blessing of v. 7b. It is *grace and peace*. Paul here sounds the most foundational words of the gospel. That gift is not remote from the doxology of the angels in Luke 2:14, even if the actual words are not parallel. And the words are clearly paralleled in the Old Testament benediction of Numbers 6: The Lord . . . be *gracious* . . . and give you *peace*.

In all three cases the news is the incursion of grace and peace into a world that yearns for them. These words catch the whole message of the gospel, better understood if we consider the antithesis, the way so many live their lives. Not to be blessed with grace means to live a life of calculation and merit, quid pro quo, and therefore a life of unending anxiety, for we never earn enough to be safe. Not to be blessed by peace means to be assigned an existence of chaos, disorder, and vexation. The opposite of grace and peace, merit and chaos, are our fate without this new beginning with this new name. This blessing from Paul, like that of Numbers 6, means to refute and override a deathly, destructive way of existence, to begin life at a different, new point.

One other extrapolation from this convergence of texts might be in order. The texts are not explicit, but there are sufficient things that point toward a life of worship, an appeal to the sacrificial, sacramental system of the temple. The priestly blessing of Numbers 6 is obviously in a context of temple activity looking toward preparation for tabernacle worship. The gospel narrative ends with purification and circumcision of Jesus in the temple. The Pauline linkage is not self-evident. But if we ask what is the payoff for the new life in the gospel, we could not do better than to read through to Rom. 12:1–2:

> present your bodies as a living sacrifice, holy and acceptable to God, which is your spiritual worship . . . that you may prove what is the will of God, what is good and acceptable and perfect.

The language is cultic. It concerns right offering. The contrast of "conform/transform" is presented in cultic language (v. 2). But the language of cult is only a vehicle for a radical evangelical offer of transformation which permits a genuinely new life. So the three texts invite a transformation at the beginning of the year, a transformation wrought by submitting to the name of this new Lord. When we do not submit to the new name, we are destined to stay in conformity to the old names which offer neither grace nor peace.

All three texts, I submit, mean to offer a genuinely new life:

Numbers 6—the blessed depart in peace, not chaos.

Luke 2—the shepherds return in doxology, not despair.

Romans 1—the church in Rome is set in a new world of peace and grace, not grudge and chaos.

When we see this convergence, we are close to a sermon which makes these affirmations:

1. These texts match our situation of beginning a new year. They propose a new beginning in which the power of the gospel is not a conclusion at the end, but the premise for all that follows.
2. The heart of the new year is that the name of Jesus has been uttered and embraced, thus establishing new identity and new vocation.
3. The new life given in the gospel is one of peace, grace, and praise, all elements in a transformed life.

These texts provide the ground for the church community to order its life afresh. The theological base is not elaborate or complicated. The name of Jesus, dead and now raised to power, is linked to our names. Our lives may now be bound to that new power unleashed in the world.

The Second Sunday After Christmas

Lutheran	Roman Catholic	Episcopal	Pres/UCC/Chr	Meth/COCU
Isa. 61:10—62:3	Sir. 24:1–4, 8–12	Jer. 31:7–14	Isa. 60:1–5	Jer. 31:7–14 or Sir. 24:1–2, 8–12
Eph. 1:3–6, 15–18	Eph. 1:3–6, 15–18	Eph. 1:3–6, 15–19a	Rev. 21:22—22:2	Rev. 21:22—22:2
John 1:1–18	John 1:1–18 or John 1:1–5, 9–14	Matt. 2:13–15, 19–23 or Luke 2:41–52 Matt. 2:1–12	Luke 2:21–24	John 1:1–18

These are three rather odd texts to hold together. The situation is more problematic because two selections are fragmented parts of longer poems, so that it is difficult to sense the flow and focus of the text. And the situation is not made any easier by this being a late (Second Sunday) reflection on Christmas. Even if this Sunday draws very close to the high festival of Epiphany, the practical reality is that much of the church is already wearied of Christmas or has returned to more "realistic" matters. In a quite specific way, these texts speak about the enduring flow that derives from Christmas, that continues to signify a changed world in which to live.

The context and immediate address of these three texts are, in each case, very different. The Old Testament reading concerns the jubilant expectation of those returned from exile who anticipate a recon-structed Jerusalem. The epistle reading is the most profound vision offered in the Pauline corpus concerning the church's participation in the promised new age. The Gospel reading is the most exquisite state-ment we have linking the person of Jesus to the eternal purposes and realities of God. So the texts in turn speak about the new *Jerusalem,* the *church* in God's cosmic action, and *Jesus* as the linchpin of new creation.

It strikes one immediately that none of these texts is descriptive. None of them speaks about what can be seen and touched and han-dled. So there is not much to be done by way of contextual analysis except to observe where the texts are placed (1) in exile, (2) among sojourners and aliens, (3) in a world of darkness. It is evident that the texts speak dramatically against their situations and for an alternative reality. That is, they portray a set of realities, assured by God, that contradicts what is presently experienced and taken for granted. They invite the listening community to align itself with the new world evoked by the text against the old world of exile, alienation, and darkness that seems overwhelming.

THE ALTERNATIVE REALITY

The texts undertake a most problematic task. They seek to open our fatigued perception of reality to a new world. That task requires a lyrical mode of speech. I do not think that the lyrical quality of all three texts is an unimportant or accidental matter. The preacher must take account of this form of expression as a crucial element in exegesis and preaching. The word to be preached after the glow of Christmas is a word powerful in its challenge to our presumed world and exquisite in its assuring characterization of an alternative.

The lyrical quality is necessary because what is promised here is unreasonable, that is, irrational, judged by the reason of the day. The texts invite the congregation to participate in an act of unreason, to entertain thoughts, to perceive reality, and even to act in ways which the world judges to be irrational.

Observe that the tone of this unreason is not angry, fearful, anxious, or desperate. It is remarkably buoyant. It is confident and upbeat, precisely because it knows that God's promises are strong and will prevail, even if we do not know how. The purpose of this sermon is to invite the congregation into this enduring promise and so to provide the congregation with reason, power, and energy to step out of the "real world" of alienation and darkness and into a different, better world. The texts assume that human persons and especially this believing community are capable of such an act of liberated imagination.

The preacher must think through how much of this can be faithfully articulated. Juan Luis Segundo, in his book *The Hidden Motives of Pastoral Action,* suggests that we have such an unconvincing gospel because of our fear and insecurity, which work in every dimension of our life. Our "hidden motive," says he, is that we are worried about ourselves, about others, and about the truth of the gospel because we can scarcely view our life according to these promises. No doubt that is a common pathology. The result is a gospel proclamation that is toned down, safe, and reasonable. But such a way is incongruent with these texts.

So we must decide in preaching, not how to persuade the congregation of this lyrical alternative, but how we ourselves can credit this alternative as more authoritative than other, more visible claims in our life. We do know, in our moments of honest acknowledgment, that the truth of the gospel comes lyrically and no other way. That is, our faith at its best is *sung.* And when we reduce that lyrical quality to prosaic "explanation" in order to control, we are left with innocuous claims. The task with these texts cannot be to persuade reasonably but only to let the texts have their own powerful, poetic say.

OLD TESTAMENT READING

In light of that key challenge for communication, we may now consider some common things in these texts:

The Isaiah reading is about joy over *newness* (61:10–62:3). This joy is comparable to a bridegroom all dressed up for the special day (61:10). Or it is the ecstasy of the bride. Of course to all other members of the wedding party, things never seem quite that buoyant, overwhelming, or important. Some of those are cynical. Some are even in tears. But the poet does not appeal to them to characterize this hope. They never get into the poem. For these two in love this is a moment like no other, never before, never again.

The joy is about newness, a new name, a moment of royal splendor, an occasion for rising out of poverty, despair, and hopelessness. The glow of the occasion, like the lingering glow of Christmas, concerns the metaphors of "brightness," "burning torch," "glory" (62:1–2). Our best metaphor for this is *light,* hence the glow. Here the poet appeals to cultic language. The Old Testament has no adequate way to speak about the glory of God, the royal power that rules wherever it is present, so it prefers the metaphor *light.* This is not because the language is limited but because this affirmation outruns the range of every language. This is why religious art features halos and streams of light as the best signals for the intrusion of God's presence. That is why on Epiphany we say a "light to the nations"; we have no better sign for such a decisive change.

Our text is about *joy at a time of light,* a light that changes everything, bringing with it the possibility of new life in a world caught in hopelessness. The text affirms that God will work a genuine newness that lets shabby, poverty-stricken Jerusalem function as a city of well-being, a gift given by the faithfulness of God.

EPISTLE READING

Ephesians 1 lacks that kind of specificity. We do not know with any precision what the situation is. But clearly the text wants the church to get its mind off itself and think about the large promises of God that surpass the church. The text announces that God has a dream that the whole world will unite, in one coherent, harmonious body. The situation addressed is the present divisions of all sorts but specifically the division between Jews and Gentiles (cf. 2:14–16). In this epistle, that division stands as a focal point for the various divisions that Paul enumerates more specifically in Gal. 3:28.

The text begins with a claim about Jesus (vv. 3–14). But it moves quickly to the church, "us" (v. 4). The church is destined by God to participate in the move toward oneness. There is a chance here to glimpse for a moment the ultimate purpose of the church, that this congregation, often marked by fear and contention and fatigue, is in fact a participant, even an agent, in the unity of all the diverse elements of creation. That is frequently hard to catch in a church which is safely homogeneous, by class or by race or by political posture, but this vision is of a community of all sorts of people gathered only around the gospel and around nothing else.

As this text is related to the Old Testament reading, we may identify three motifs in vv. 17–18. First, the God who works in the event of Jesus is the "Father of glory." While we need not linger over the troubled metaphor of "Father," we stress that this God is the one "of glory," that is, the one who administers the light that will change the world. And this "Father of glory" sends this light to "enlighten the eyes of our hearts" so that our hearts may see and notice and decide differently. The hearts of believers, bathed in the light, are permitted to see what the world does not see (Matt. 11:25–27). What we may see, when illuminated by the glory, is that the world is not hatefully divided into Jews and Gentiles. It is not fiercely divided into Russians and Americans or any of the other pseudodivisions on which we use so much energy.

Our hearts are opened by the glory to a new discernment, to see behind and before our imagined divisions that by the mercy of God we are bound to each other in ways that override our divisions. The Emmaus Homes for the handicapped people in my church have as a slogan "These residents are more like us than different from us." That statement is hard to believe because the differences seem so obvious and the divisions are daily reenforced by fear, hatred, propaganda, and self-interest. But to participate in those imagined and contrived divisions is to betray and disregard the Father of light, who in Jesus has made it a different kind of world.

Finally in v. 18, the text invites us to be aware that we are called to "the hope." We are not, first of all, called to a mission or to a work, or to a stewardship campaign, or even to a peace rally or whatever. We are *called to the hope*. And the substance of the hope is the unity of all creation, which belongs to God, against all our little postures of division. What a vocation—to be a community that knows for sure, embodies in its life, and shows in its interaction that the hope is already a sure reality!

Only a poet could move from *the governance of light to the hope of unity,* but that is what this text claims. The light of this God creates a new reality on earth. The light is not divisible. It shines everywhere from the throne of God. That irresistible reality makes evident that our divisions are fraudulent. We are the ones who do not doubt that this hope is the deepest reality we know.

GOSPEL READING

The third text (John 1:1–18) is so well-known that we almost miss its grandeur. This text wants us for an instant to think back behind time to the moment of creation. In that moment a word was uttered. In that moment a light was given. The word of life and the light of unity have been present to the world since that instant. It is not as though later on God devised a strategy to overcome a problem. From the very beginning it has been God's singular purpose to hold the thing together, to bind it into a oneness where God's own rule is established and God's purpose fully celebrated.

In that respect this text is not different from the others. It too is about the overriding light of God that issues in glory in the world. It shines everywhere. The force of darkness, real as it is, cannot rival it. Then this text moves to a specific embodiment of the light. It dares to affirm that in this Jesus, the one whose birth we celebrate, all this glory has come to concrete presence, and we are invited to be dazzled at the scandal. Or we may be offended by it. When we see the person of Jesus, we are clear on the eternal purpose God has for creation. When we witness again the Christmas pageant, we witness the drama whereby the dark places of life are brought under the rule of God. And, by this concrete gift among us, we are empowered and permitted to become children of this God who loves us more than we can love ourselves. We are invited to have done with our life of darkness. It is made clear that we no longer have to live as though the world is hostile, as though we must look after our own well-being, for that has all been secured in this one for whom the world, both Jewish and Gentile, has waited.

When the epistle and Gospel reading are held together, one observes that if we are to be "children of God," it makes us children of the "Father of glory," that is, "children of light" who no longer have to work our fearful, destructive way in the darkness.

The claims of these texts are not, in broad outline, difficult to trace. To be sure, the metaphors are elusive and have considerable depth, and therefore we do not presume to have explored them in any depth. But the real problem in preaching here is not to "speak the claim." It is rather to provide help in understanding how these texts might *function* in one's life. What is one to do with such visionary articulation? It all seems splendid, but it also seems quite remote from where we must live. The sermon, I submit, must attend to the pastoral help that is needed in embracing the new reality.

The new world presented here needs to be seen in its ecstatic purity, unencumbered by any "realism." The Christian gospel does indeed hold decisively to a new world coming. This is not otherworldly escape. It is thisworldly. But it is also not "realized eschatology" in any complacent sense. The world envisioned here is the kingdom of God, free of the scars of death, with which we daily contend. The congregation may be helped to see the pure vision because after a while we all become tired and frustrated and probably persuaded out of the vision. This is a time for clarifying the vision and reclaiming it, so that we do not forget in all the dailiness what we are up to.

The characterization of this gift of light has as one of its spinoffs a fresh disclosure about this old world we inhabit. Almost in passing, these texts portray the darkness. And this is not unimportant, for we grow cynically accustomed to it. After a while we do not notice. We easily accommodate so much that is incongruent with this great hope. So this sermon might help people discover with honesty our sense of dismay at the world as it is. These texts ask that we stay alert, even raw, about how it really is. Just now the darkness touches us in terms of failed economics, of frenzied nuclear pursuit, of disintegrated social existence. These factors—economic, nuclear, social—are more deathly than our ideologies and propaganda would have us realize. The economy does destroy people. Nuclear war cannot be won. We must not be soothed about these matters. Christians who hope actively for the new world of light are invited to look honestly into the old reality, not to lie about it, not to withdraw from it, but to face it fully and then to decide that the light has more truth than the darkness. We may reshape our life for the sake of the light.

The power of this season requires that the congregation face the deep contrast and discontinuity between the shabby world of brokenness (darkness) and the new world of light. They are drastically different. They are not so related to each other that one may be derived from the other. We do not know how to get from the one to the other. The Bible asserts, but it does not explain and does not provide a step-by-step process. We are not given a routing. These poets speak our yearning to receive the new world and our resolve to move toward it, even at cost. In the preaching moment, the linkage is left to rhetoric, to drama, to imagination, where God's Spirit may lead us. The preacher does not need to become a scribal explainer. It is enough to speak the vision with clarity and to invite believers to embrace the light and therefore to quit the darkness.

The task of preaching here is that the word brings to speech the alternative. The "Father of glory" begins to move in on our old age. In this moment of special communication, the light dawns, not just on our ears by the spoken word; it begins to open our imaginations. The grip of the old rhetoric and of the fearful ideology that traps us begins to loosen. It could happen that we become aware that the promise is already being kept. The child has been born. The light has shown. We are already new children of God. The eyes of our hearts have been enlightened.

We begin tentatively to live in the new world, to trust the hope ordained among us. It could happen that we begin to live in new ways, seeing "beyond the tears" the new Jerusalem, noting that the binding unity of the Creator overrides our fearful divisions. We turn loose our resentful world and live anew. The epiphany is not a cognitive event. It is deeply transformative of our common life. These texts offer that much.

To speak it truly, the preacher should himself/herself be deeply fascinated by the new invitation now confronting us. It could be the wedding day for the whole community of grooms and brides on our way, rejoicing.